A LIFE IN A DAY

Soviet Life; Brutal, Mundane and Sublime

Hilkka Polvinen Mednis

**Published in May 2022 by emp3books Ltd
6 Silvester Way, Church Crookham, Fleet,
GU52 0TD**

©Russell Connor 2022

ISBN: 9781910734476

This is a work of fiction. All the main characters come from the imagination of Hilkka Polvinen Mednis, who is also a work of fiction.

The right of Russell John Connor to be identified as the author of this work has been asserted in accordance with sections 77 and 78 of the Copyright Designs and Patents Act 1988.

First published in Russian in 2004 by Smirnova Modern Classics.

CONTENTS

About the Author

Hilkka Mednis (née Polvinen) was born in Finland in 1927. One of five daughters of Pauli and Anne Polvinen, she enjoyed a happy early childhood until her mother died in childbirth. Then, at the age of thirteen, on the invasion of Finland by the Red Army, she, together with her father and three of her sisters were deported to Siberia. Despite the cruel conditions, all the family members survived and, on the 28th August, 1948, Hilkka married Janis Mednis, a young Latvian who had also been deported. Janis died in a great crush of people when both attended Stalin's funeral in 1953. Hilkka survived and bore his child. However, she suffered from what would now be called anxiety disorder and post-natal depression.

In 1970, she was given permission to relocate to Leningrad with her son, Pavel, who was granted a scholarship at the prestigious Vaganova Ballet School in the city. There she shared a small apartment with her mother-in-law. Hilkka lived to the age of seventy-two and was survived by her second husband, Aleksey Alkohov, who was a well-known actor.

A Life in a Day is translated from Russian by Hilkka's step-daughter, Alina Freeman who now lives in Massachusetts, USA.

September 21st, 1996 – St. Petersburg

In 1978 I sent a manuscript of my book, *A Life in a Day,* to a number of publishers and literary journals in Moscow and Leningrad. I had only one reply and I quote it in full:

Esteemed Comrade Mednis,
My sincerest thanks for sending Smirnova Press[1] your manuscript. I read it with interest and consider it to have significant literary merit. In its title and style, it reminds me of Solzhenitsyn's 'One Day in the Life of Ivan Denisovich'. Despite the above, I regret to inform you that we will not be publishing your book and I return the manuscript forthwith.

When we received your work, I contemplated two options, ignore it or report it. However, given the quality of your work and the sincerity with which you write, I have decided to respond to you, although, it is only to instruct you not to send this work to any other publisher. Expressing anti-Soviet sentiment is a very serious matter.

There may be a time and a place for all things, but this is not the time or place for your book.

However, I would be happy to consider anything else

---

[1] Smirnova Press. Publishers based in Moscow.

that you write as you clearly have talent.

Always at your service

Sergei Barovchatov

I have not written anything since and so had no further contact with Barovchatov. This remains my only book and is unpublished.

Now, many years on, I am putting my affairs in order. I don't want to leave behind any mess for people to sort out when I have gone. Maybe those who happen to stumble upon my work in the future will think that the time is right to publish it, but it won't be in my lifetime.

So much has changed. We can write without censorship but who is interested in the past? Everyone is so keen to talk of tomorrow, of the bright future in a democratic Russia, travelling, making money and becoming rich. I doubt whether anyone wants to look back. But, one day they might. Maybe?

I am attaching this letter to the manuscript.

Editor's Note

In the normal course of publishing a book, the editor suggests revisions and, I like to think, the collaboration between editor and author improves the finished article. Now that the author of *A Life in a Day* is no longer with us, this collaborative process has not been possible. Without Hilkka's input we have decided to publish the book as it was written without redaction. I have limited my involvement to helping foreign readers by adding some notes of explanation to the text and a postscript.

Were she still with us, I would have suggested to the author that she adds more of her time spent in Siberia and I would have asked her to provide a little more detail of her family tree. It took me some time to understand that Hilkka's father, a widower, married her deceased husband's mother who was also a widow. But this is nit-picking. The book is raw and real. It is about life; hard, Soviet life. It is also about overcoming adversity, trauma, loss, anxiety and depression and doing so without the use of medication or professional therapy. Now it is published. It is her time and place.

Translator's Note

I have been granted the honour and privilege of translating my stepmother's work. It has been an opportunity to remember her, together with my father, and to reconnect with a past that, now, seems such a long time ago.

I first met Hilkka when she came to visit Father at his apartment in Leningrad. I can see her now with her blonde hair, big blue eyes, round face and distinct cheekbones. Her face had the quality of a friendly, china doll, accentuated by porcelain skin. Initially, she appeared shy but once you got to know Hilkka you discovered tremendous depth of character and she shared my father's ironic take on life.

I can really say that Father and Hilkka were a couple in love, and, even when filming took my father off to far-flung parts of the Soviet Union, they were rarely separated.

The role as the Tsar in *The Kaiser and I* confirmed my father as a great character actor. In the early-eighties, he starred in some iconic Russian films; funny, whimsical and romantic. After these he was recognised where ever he went and I often joked with him that he was world famous in the Soviet Union.

As an actor who had become a nation's favourite, my

father was able to maintain a rather good lifestyle and he and Hilkka entertained friends and acquaintances both in their city apartment and at their dacha. Hilkka proved to be a great cook and hostess. However, as the 1980's progressed, the appetite for the sort of film my father typically starred in lessened and his acting career faded. Luckily, he was happy to retire to the countryside with Hilkka.

Times change, and, to the surprise of most Russians, the Soviet Union collapsed in 1991. Actually, it was as shocking to many as if the sun had suddenly risen in the west. Old certainties and securities were removed, and, at first, there was an economic collapse with the change of regime. Petty crime, such as stealing clothes off washing lines and vegetables off allotments, turned into more serious ones and when valuables were stolen from Father's St. Petersburg apartment we thought that Hilkka's manuscript had been lost forever, as it was in a missing box along with some jewellery.

Fate, it seems, delivered a strange twist as the manuscript, somehow, was found at a market stall and was returned to the publisher who originally refused to publish the book.

With the newfound freedoms, I took the opportunity to travel and met my husband to be in the USA. I now live in Massachusetts and with all my worldly possessions and freedom I sometimes wake up wondering if my life in the Soviet Union ever existed. Thankfully, *A Life in a Day* reminds me of some of the highs and lows of living in those times.

Alina Freeman

5.15am

I half expected the visit. No, in truth I fully expected it and, in fact, I'd been expecting it most of my adult life. Only, when it came I was deep within a recurring dream and the banging on the door, at first, added to the soundtrack. 'Is that you Misha?' A familiar voice pulled my body out of itself and the cloaked pursuant in my dream retreated into the shadows, prepared to visit again on another occasion. Someone, insistently, was demanding entry. I grabbed my dressing gown, stood into my slippers and shouted, 'Who is it?' but I knew the answer before I heard, 'State Security.'

The apartment door, restrained by the security chain, cracked open and the tell-tale red band on the cap confirmed the identity of the shadowy figure outside. A tremor started in my fingers and began to work its way up my arm as I let the officer and two of his associates into my cramped room - along with the smell of a thousand old cigarettes. 'Hilkka Mednis?' The leader's nicotine voice was a low growl.

　　　'Yes.'

　　　'Get dressed. You are to come with me.'

　　　'Where to?' There was no answer but I knew it was the Big House.[2]

---

[2] The Big House (Bolshoy Dom in Russian) was the Leningrad headquarters of the Committee for State

'Get dressed.'

'Is that you Misha?' The constant question came from the bedroom. Even at this unearthly hour, my mother-in-law's voice was surprisingly strong.

'Svetlana, don't worry. I'm just going out, back soon.' I called out in as reassuring voice as I could muster. I knew that she would soon go back to sleep and later would have no recollection of any early morning callers. 'You will have to wait outside whilst I dress.' I addressed the Officer and he looked around the rooms - probably to see if there were any other exits.

'Be quick.' He turned and ushered the men out.

The bedside clock showed that it was five-seventeen. Darkness and the early hours were the perfect working conditions for these tradesmen.

I was aware of my high pulse and beating heart and forced myself to focus on practicalities. Who would get Svetlana her breakfast? How could I let the Institute know that I would be late for work? What did I need to buy on the way home for the evening meal? I was surprised that my thoughts were so structured even if they did not address the reason for the KGB's early morning call. I pulled on yesterday's clothes, which lay scatted on a chair and, with

---

Security (KGB) until the collapse of the Soviet Union.

shaking hands, struggled to do up the buttons on my cardigan.

Wrapping a scarf around the collar of my winter coat, I stepped out of the room. It was clear that the banging had awoken the neighbours as lights shone from under the closed doors. I could almost see them pressed up against the door, straining to hear any clues as to the purpose of the visit and hoping that we were the only ones the KGB were visiting that night.

As we left the building, I glimpsed the face of Mrs. Morozova at her window before she hurriedly hid behind the thick curtains. A nasty smile seemed to play on her lips. Soon, the block's inveterate gossiper would ensure that everyone would know that Hilkka Mednis had been hauled off to the Big House.

Gorokhovaya Street was empty. No passing feet had yet disturbed the frosted pavement. A biting wind headed up from the Neva and we all instinctively pulled up collars and nestled into coats. The Zhiguli opposite seemed to pulse gently under dim streetlights that swung from the cables down the middle of the boulevard.

Sitting in the back seat of the car next to the officer and, separated from home and in the company of strangers, I could feel fear. Literally, I had the sensation of cold, crawling fear work its way up my body from the toes. With it, I felt that I was rising in my seat, my head extended as if to force its way through the roof, my body trying to climb out of itself, mind whirling. For a moment, I wondered whether I was still in my dream and this officer was my pursuant.

The car started, the wheels span on the dirty snow piled by the roadside, and, gathering speed, it seemed to strain to breaking the car's suspension on the cobbled boulevard. The jolting shook my mind as if it was lemonade in a bottle. Questions bubbled up. *Why? What had I done? Who had denounced me? What was going to happen? Who can help?* After a short ride to the Big House, I was sweaty despite the lack of heating.

I knew the Big House well. That is, I had passed it every day on my way to work. Its monumental style was out of place amongst Leningrad's classical form and I had never liked it and that was not just because of its use by the KGB. It was bleak and austere; a brute amongst its pastel coloured and colonnaded neighbours. Stories about what went on in the Big House were common talking points in trusted company. I was always amused by the grim saying that from the basement you could see all the way to Siberia. I had never before, though, been inside.

Despite there being large double doors at the front,

4

opening into what looked like an impressive foyer, I was escorted through, what amounted to, a side entrance and into a dimly-lit hallway with a sleepy-looking guard sitting in a booth protected by lattice ironworks. The head of the escort announced himself but I didn't catch his name properly and was immediately led along a corridor. I was frightened, but movement seemed to keep the rising panic from completely overwhelming me.

I let out an audible gasp, and felt weak at the knees, when we turned and headed downstairs. In such a tall, imposing building, with its associated tenants, there is something truly dreadful in heading to the basement. I was expecting to see a row of cells but we entered another corridor with what looked like ordinary office doors stretching to infinity.

After passing a few doors, I was made to halt whilst one was unlocked and I was ordered through. 'Wait here,' was the only instruction and I was left alone in a small, dingy room dimly lit by a single bulb hanging, un-shaded, from a low ceiling. There was just enough room for a table and three chairs, and at the top of one wall were small opaque windows, which presumably were at street level. I slumped onto one of the chairs and put my head in my hands. What to do?

My main concern was to stem the fear that literally pulsated, pumped and whirred in my brain. If I didn't, I knew that I could easily tip into a familiar state of over over-whelming anxiety. I remembered the things that I had learnt to keep my mind under control. Breathe deeply, sit upright, move, certainly don't slump, focus on what is happening now, on what is around me. I looked around the room to help me to take my mind off my inner state, but the metal chairs with their chipped paint and the metal table bolted to the floor gave no positive impressions to work with.

Gradually, I pulled back from the precipice of panic and my heart rate reduced. The pressure in my head eased. I took consolation that I had something to fear. In the past I had felt intense anxiety and panic for the slightest of reasons. At those times I felt I was a woman on the edge of insanity. At least here, I had a reason to feel as I did. Being in the clutches of the KGB was truly frightening.

I speculated again on why I had been brought here at such an ungodly hour. Was it Mrs. Morozova denouncing me for playing tango music on my old record player? Unlikely; such small transgressions were not of interest to the KGB anymore. Was it because someone had informed them of my impersonation of Brezhnev[3]? I recalled the time that I

---

[3] Leonid Ilyich Brezhnev was the General Secretary of the Communist Party of the Soviet Union from 1964 to his death in 1982. He was the subject of many

had imitated his way of speaking; pronounced sausages instead of socialism. But I had been amongst friends at one of our occasional after-work parties and we all told Brezhnev related jokes. Was it because of the broken copier at work? Surely not! I hadn't touched it, and, anyway, that was not KGB business. As nothing I had done made sense, I understood that something had happened to my son, Pavel. The previous week I had waved goodbye to him at Pulkovo airport before he set off with the Kirov Ballet on their tour of England and USA. Had he been hurt? I speculated, But why the KGB?

I was left to speculate on the cause and I was left to speculate on the reason for being kept waiting for such a long time. I sat on one of the metal chairs, icy cold to the touch, and fidgeted but failed to get comfortable. I had to resort to getting up, taking a few paces, and sitting down again. With no means of telling the time I guessed it must have been at least two hours before I heard footsteps down the corridor. However, they passed my door and I knew that I was being softened up for something. *Probably standard practice,* I thought, *why else pull me out of bed and*

---

private jokes especially as a war wound to his jaw made his pronunciation difficult at times. Also, his declining health and habit of drinking to excess provided a number of unusual mannerisms and amusing incidents.

then have me hang around?

After a while, I remembered the after-work party where I had impersonated Brezhnev and recalled the joke I had also told. It was the one where Brezhnev scolds his speechwriter for giving him a speech that lasted forty-five minutes when he only wanted one that lasted fifteen. The speechwriter replied that he gave him three copies. If I was to do a seven-year stretch for telling political jokes, at least it was a good one.

When the handle of the door turned, I jumped and shivered uncontrollably as another KGB officer in their distinctive uniform entered the room.

My interrogator, as he turned out to be, was a thin man with a pale and bony face, protruding eyes and big, fleshy lips. As he stood opposite and stared down at me I noticed that he had very scaly skin especially above his eyebrows and his right eye squinted away as if looking at a feature on the wall to my left. Surely this was a face that had provoked merciless bullying at school and was now that of a man who found solace in the strong arms of the KGB. He did not introduce himself but I felt that he would be less intimidating if I thought of him as The Lizard.

　'Name?' The Lizard demanded.
　'Hilkka Mednis.'
　'Patronym?'
　'Paulievna.'

'Maiden name?'

'Polvinen.'

'Date of birth?'

'1st June, 1927.'

'Place of birth?' I wanted to say, 'Independent Finland' but I knew that I must not antagonise The Lizard or create any more tension in my already overloaded state.

'Karelia.' I muttered.

'Place of work?'

'Institute of Microbiology.'

'Name of son?' The Lizard's one good eye was fixed on me and I knew that this was something to do with Pavel.

'Pavel Mednis.'

'Have you had any contact with your son since he flew to England?'

'No. No, not at all.' The Lizard glared at me.

'Why did you not inform us before he left that he was going to defect?'

'Defect!' My heart boomed and I felt as if bats were released into my chest.

'Yes, defect.' The Lizard banged his hand down on the table. 'He is a traitor. Don't lie to me. If you knew he was going to defect this is a serious crime... as is associating with a traitor.'

'I... I didn't know.' I must have been barely audible. I could hardly think let alone speak.

'Who radicalised him?'

'I don't know what you mean.'

'Of course you do.' The Lizard emphasised his

9

shouted assertion by slapping the palms of his hands together. The bats took flight again. 'Of course you do. The West is degenerate, immoral and dangerous. They have no discipline. Someone must have turned his mind, persuaded him that the glitter was real.'

'I don't know of anyone... I had no idea.'

'Do you know Oleg Vasiliev?'

'Yes... he's a friend of Pavel.'

'Did he radicalise him?'

'But, but he is simply a flatmate, friend, fellow student from the Vaganova[4]. Both are at the Kirov.[5]' I didn't add, 'and are lovers.'

'What of Professor Nikolyukin?'

'What of him?

'Don't be smart with me. Did he radicalise your son?'

'No. Not at all. Pavel worshipped his old teacher and mentor.'

The Lizard listed more names with the same intention and the stupidity of it eased my nerves slightly. I breathed a little more easily and the beating of the bats' wings lessened. Eventually, he stopped and finished with, 'Comrade Mednis, think about it.' With this, he left the room. I could not

---

[4] Established in 1738, The Vaganova Academy of Russian Ballet is a school of classical ballet in St. Petersburg, Russia.

[5] Kirov Ballet. This is the Soviet name for the Marriinsky Ballet.

think; it was as if a bus had hit me and all I could do was keep still until help arrived. Help, of course, didn't arrive, but after forty minutes or so I felt that, at least, the shock wasn't going to tip me over the edge. I did, though, understand that defection was a very serious matter and when my thoughts cleared a little I wondered whether the authorities still set out to kill traitors abroad? Brezhnev may have visited New York but the West was still the enemy.

I thought of Pavel and his friend in London. *Something must have happened, something urgent and unplanned. Something about their relationship must have got out. Something extraordinary must have occurred for him not to want to return.* He had definitely not planned it, that I was sure of. I had helped him pack his bag and he hadn't taken anything to indicate he wasn't coming back. His little bear mascot, which he had since a young child was left on his pillow and, with the hugs at the airport, there had been no strange or out of place comment; simply excitement and promises of a safe return. Pavel wasn't good at telling lies or keeping secrets from me.

Just as the reality was sinking in that I might not see my son again, the door opened and The Lizard stepped in holding a clipboard. I wondered if I was going to be hit with it but he raised it and then slapped down on the table with the command, 'Read it.' On it was a typed letter; the words of which took

11

time to come into focus.

Pavel, my darling, you have made a terrible mistake. But it is a mistake that can easily be rectified. Present yourself at the Soviet Embassy in London. They will treat you fairly. Your life is here in Leningrad with the Kirov and the people who love you. To think that we may never see each other again. That is too much.

If you do not present yourself to the Soviet Authorities, you will be treated as a traitor, the sentence for which is execution.

After I had read it, The Lizard said, 'Now write it out in your own hand, or something similar.' I didn't immediately respond and he added, 'Think on it. Think of your father and stepmother. Think of your sisters. Life could become a lot harder for them... associating with a traitor.' I wanted to correct him. My father's life couldn't be made harder. He was close to death with throat cancer. But, of course, I didn't correct him and he handed me a pen and nodded towards the blank paper in the file. With the word, 'Write,' he left the room and, after a short while, I wrote out the letter. What else to do?

The hardest part was to control the shake in my writing hand, but I managed to copy the text in reasonable order. Only, I made deliberate spelling mistakes, which I was sure Pavel would notice. I had worked hard at Russian and had become not only fluent but also perfect in spelling. This small sign would show that I had been forced to write it. I also signed it rather formally, 'Your Loving Mother,' although it was always the custom for me to sign letters to him, 'Mamma.'

The Lizard took the finished letter and read it through. He might have seen the spelling mistakes because he looked at me with some disgust in his face – foreigners! He left me alone again but soon returned and told me I was free to go but had to stay in the city. Also, if I was to hear from Pavel, I must immediately report this.

11.15am

The cold of the December day slapped me in the face as I left the Big House and my cardigan under the winter coat was insufficient to prevent a chill immediately taking hold. I tightened my scarf and stuffed my un-gloved hands deep into my pockets. At least I knew the road well and had the choice of taking the number 10 tram towards Lomonosov Street or the number 8 trolleybus towards Zagorodny Avenue although that meant a longer walk at the end. The trolleybuses were always warm and, with their upholstered seats, were surprisingly comfortable. I decided to take comfort in anyway that I could. Thankfully the whiskers of the trolleybus's electrical conductors were soon seen from afar and, once I was on board, I slumped into a free seat. I noticed that the clock above the driver said eleven-thirty. I had been in the KGB's company for about six hours but somehow it felt like a lifetime.

Now I needed again to be practical, not just to take my mind off the news that I might not see my son again, Svetlana would be up and hungry. Not only that, I had missed a morning's work without giving notice and needed to get there as soon as possible. However, it wasn't long before my thoughts returned to Pavel. As we passed Kasanskaya I mentally turned right and, in my mind, headed towards the Kirov. I wondered if Professor Nikolyukin or the Director were now being grilled about the defection. Near to the Kirov, Pavel lived with his friend, Oleg, in a small room of a hostel owned by the Kirov. In the room were two single beds and a large wardrobe and I thought of Pavel's little, lonely bear.

What had happened? I speculated. I could only think that, somehow, they had tasted a freedom that did not exist for them here. Not so much an artistic freedom; Pavel seemed happy with his roles and the progress he was making as a dancer; but sexual freedom. The couple had been discrete about their relationship. Homosexuals were common in the ballet world but outside they faced an increasingly hostile environment. Arrests were frequent and the general public's tolerance had always been low.

I thought back to Pavel's childhood and the time I took him to his first ballet at the age of seven. Even before the performance, he marvelled at the theatre's crystal chandeliers, stuccoed interior, classical murals and velvet curtains patterned with dancing lights. After the ballet he said, 'That is my life,' and, from then on, dancing was everything. I remembered when the boys in the yard pretended to be astronauts – *Izvestiya* had just reported that Russia was the first to have a man undertake a spacewalk[6] – Pavel really

---

[6] On 18 March 1965, Alexey Arkhipovich Leonov became the first human to conduct extra-vehicular activity(EVA), exiting the capsule during the Voskhod 2 mission for a 12-minute spacewalk.

looked like he knew what it would be to move in space. He had an extraordinary plastique that made him stand out from the other kids who just ran around shouting. But, he was a real boy and would be outside as much as he could with friends – even in winter.

From the moment he decided to become a ballet dancer he never put himself in any danger. Whilst other boys broke bones falling out of trees or off walls, Pavel stayed safe. He was just enough part of the gang never to be bullied but his choice to pursue ballet provided real challenges. At the Pioneers[7] the boys made fun of him but he was never completely isolated as they were impressed with the strength he showed in the military exercises, and in athletics he also excelled. He participated as little as he could in the Komsomol[8]; ballet had taken him over completely by the age of fourteen.

With the heat of the trolleybus, the emotions of the morning and my reminiscences, I suddenly felt tired,

---

[7] During the existence of the Soviet Union, thousands of Young Pioneer camps and Young Pioneer Palaces were built.
[8] The All-Union Leninist Young Communist League (usually known as Komsomol) was a political youth organisation in the Soviet Union. It promoted sports and outdoor skills and taught communist principles.

sleepy even, and I was pleased about this. In the past when my mind had started to whirl it used to become uncontrollable and was almost impossible to stop. Now it was operating at a surprisingly normal pace. In this dreamy state, I nearly missed my stop but jumped up and quickly managed to leap through the closing doors. After the super-heated luxury of the trolleybus the cold again came as a shock but I could not scurry straight home as there was not even bread and butter at home and I couldn't let Svetlana go hungry for the whole day.

The small shop near Senaya Square had a large, ragged queue outside and I asked, 'Who is the last in line?'

'I am.' A hunched-backed babushka wearing a woollen beret answered.

'What is available?'

'Bananas.'

Pulling my scarf tight, I joined the queue hoping that the biting wind might be lessened by the huddle. As I approached the counter I was disappointed to see that the bananas were green and rock-hard looking but I bought two, as I had not seen them in the shops for months. After that, I had to join another, smaller queue for the bread and butter.

Clutching my small pile of provisions, I pushed on home for its warm embrace. The communal heating in the block was temperamental, but of late, for some reason, it excelled itself and the scalding radiators pumped out pure bliss.

I didn't meet anyone on the wide staircase of our block. Only, I felt that the door of Mrs. Morozova had cracked open once I had passed. She was probably surprised and disappointed to see me back.

The main door on the third floor had been removed at the time of the sub-division and I walked down a narrow corridor to our rooms at the back of the block. Thin, badly erected walls separated families randomly thrown together through the Soviet housing policy. When I entered our rooms, the sensations never altered, I felt a heavy weight or sadness that Svetlana's family had once owned the whole floor of this classical block but now Svetlana was limited to what were the maid's small rooms. But, if I tried to talk to Svetlana about it, when she still recalled the old days, she would always say, 'I was the lucky one. So many friends and neighbours went missing or were transported to Siberia.9' 'Is that

---

9 By the request of General Secretary, N.S. Khruschev, in February 1954, an official report listed the total number of people prosecuted for counter-revolutionary crimes during the period from 1921 to 1954. During that period the Soviet authorities indicted 3,777,380 individuals, including 642,980 who received the death penalty, 2,369,220 with sentences of up to 25 years, and 765,180 exiled or

you Misha?' Svetlana called out and I assured her that her long dead husband was not the one entering.

Svetlana was sitting by her bed in a winged chair wearing a large dressing gown that engulfed her small body. The gown, thin in places, had large stains that could not be removed however much I soaked or boiled it. Her wrinkled face, the colour of faded parchment, was almost luminescent in the near darkness of her room even though she had managed to open the single curtain. Little light at the best of times penetrated the old servants' quarters, but it was especially gloomy today. The weak December sun had risen late behind snow-laden clouds and was already setting. The room also smelled of used commode. 'I hope you slept well.' I asked.

'I didn't sleep a wink.' Despite her diminutive frame, Svetlana had a strong voice.

'Are you hungry?'

'I have eaten. I made some solyanka soup and boiled potatoes.'

'Good.' I said but I knew that Svetlana hadn't ventured out of her room for over a year now.

---

deported. At the time of the report, it further stated, there were 467,946 people in the labour camps and prisons convicted for counter-revolutionary crimes and 62,462 former prisoners in exile.

I lifted the lid of the commode and took the pot to the communal toilet. On an empty stomach, I could not help feeling nauseous. Thankfully, the toilet, although old and chipped, was always spotlessly clean. Mrs. Alyokhina at 5-3c was a fastidious cleaner and once she had swept and dusted, and re-swept and re-dusted her own rooms, she turned her attention to the toilet and kitchen. She even provided the toilet paper! Her husband worked at *Leningradskaya Pravda* and a benefit of the toilet paper was that you could also catch up on recent news. It was in this small space that I learnt that the world outside of the Soviet Union was hostile and threatening, Russia was a fortress, always a target for missiles. I learnt of the amazing advances in Soviet technology and kept up to date with the space programme. I also learnt of the terrible conditions of the peasants in El Salvador and oppression of Negroes in the USA.

Every day I gave thanks to Mrs. Alyokhina for her efforts as communal facilities in the rest of the block were often far from pleasant and some were truly disgusting.

I filled a bowl and, back in my room, washed with soap and water and changed my clothes. The sweat of fear had already turned sour.

In the kitchen, I took a tin of sprats from my section

in the communal larder and made some sandwiches. Again, I gave thanks for my blessings, as, on our floor at least, no food was pilfered; not even Mrs. Stepanova's wonderful, and tempting, pickled mushrooms. I ate with Svetlana, thankfully in silence.

My unmade daybed looked inviting. I could easily have got in knowing that sleep would have come quickly but I had to get to the Institute. The Academician whom I worked for did not look on lateness and unauthorised absence favourably. Before I left, I told Svetlana that I would be back later and then looked around our rooms. It never failed to strike me how many pictures hung on the walls in the tiny, cramped space. It was as if, in 1917, the whole floor had been tipped up and all the artwork slid into these rooms. As the paintings were largely from the end of the nineteenth century, they were dark and the effect added to the claustrophobic quality.

1.00pm

Before setting off to the Institute, I dressed properly this time and took a felt hat and thick mittens with me. The wind had not ceased and now carried stinging ice crystals. I was thankful that I didn't need to wait long for a tram. Their frequency continually amazed me in a city where electricity cuts were common and many basic provisions were in short supply. With this wind, I was especially pleased to see the tram's snub nose trundle into view

As it was early afternoon I managed to get a prime seat above one of the heaters. The window was opaque with frosted dirt but I didn't need to see out; I knew the journey precisely. There were eight stops to the Institute and then a short walk. Normally, I would think of the day ahead but, at that moment, I didn't want to think at all. However, I reflected on my own thinking and was pleased I maintained a relative calmness, which I didn't want to spoil. In the past, my thoughts could flock like starlings in autumn and the murmurations could be wild and unpredictable.

Despite trying to concentrate on the here and now; the capped and scarved heads of fellow passengers, the announcements of the next stop, the blast of cold air with every clack of the opening and closing doors, my thoughts turned to Pavel. *Now I will not be washing and ironing his training leotards and vests.* I thought. It was a job I enjoyed, and, although they were always stained and sweaty, they always smelled sweet to me. A mother's nose I suppose. *I will never again go to the dress rehearsals of the new productions. I will never talk animatedly to him about his roles and how he might interpret these even though they were mostly minor ones.* He was not yet an 'etoile' but had the ambition to dance the major solo roles.

I again thought of Professor Nikolyukin. *Would he suffer the same fate as old Professor Pushkin[10]?* Hounded by the KGB after Nureyev[11] and Baryshnikov[12] defected, Pushkin had become a

---

[10] Acclaimed teacher at the Vaganova.

[11] Nureyev; Rudolf Nureyev (1938 to 1993) had his early career with the Kirov Ballet. He defected from the Soviet Union to the West in 1961, despite KGB efforts to stop him. This was the first defection of a Soviet artist during the Cold War and it created an international sensation. He went on to dance with The Royal Ballet in London and from 1983 to 1989 served as director of the Paris Opera Ballet.

[12] Baryshnikov; Mikhail Baryshnikov (1948 to present) is a Latvian-born Russian and Canadian dancer, choreographer and actor. After a promising start in the Kirov Ballet, Baryshnikov defected to Canada in 1974 for more opportunities in Western dance.

physical and emotional wreck. *Did Pavel understand the impact his action would have on others? Had Nureyev influenced Pavel?* I knew Nureyev danced at Covent Garden. Maybe he had turned the young men's minds? I felt an anger building towards him, who I had only heard of, and then chastised myself. *Maybe the immoral and decadent West gave them room to be free?* I pondered. *Wouldn't any mother want their son to live in a society that accepted them for who they were?*

I understood that I had to control my speculations for now and turned my attention to what I would say to my boss. *Maybe I could just say that Svetlana has been ill? Yet, why had I not telephoned?* Anyway, it would soon become common knowledge that Pavel had defected and I decided to tell the truth.

I normally enjoyed my short walk to the Institute of Microbiology but today I pulled down my hat and headed as fast as I could from the trolley-bus stop to work. Concentrating on missing the large patches of ice covering the dirty puddles provided a few minutes of blessed relief from thinking about the morning.

The Institute sat within its own grounds and extensive laboratories lay behind the main building. I had to show my pass to the security officer at the gate and again at reception. My forced, cheery, 'Hello,' to Valentina, who sat behind a grand desk, was met with an unusually sullen response. When I stepped into the big office of the Academician I feared that news of Pavel's defection preceded me. Propped against my typewriter was a note addressed, 'Comrade Mednis'. I took off my winter coat and stuffed the hat and gloves in the pocket before taking hold of the envelope. In it there was a handwritten note demanding, 'See me at once.' It was written in the hand of my boss, Professor Lebedev, Academician and Head of Bacterial Science.

I knocked on Professor Lebedev's door and waited for the command of, 'Come.' When I entered his office, I immediately thought how brutish he looked with his closely cropped hair. Although over sixty, he liked to keep fit and was a vain man who was always checking his moustache in a mirror. I waited silently and then he stood up. Without making eye contact, he stretched out his hand with a letter in it and said, 'We had a visit today.' I guessed immediately what was in the letter and, initially, struggled to focus on the dancing words on the page. Then I read:

Comrade Mednis,

As from 15th December 1976, your employment is terminated at the Institute of Microbiology.

Staff reduction is the reason.

You will be paid up until the 24th December.

Signed

My first thought was 24th December - Merry Christmas![13] Then I looked at him and could feel tears forming. *Be strong, don't let him know what a blow this is to you.*

'Sorry...' The Professor sounded, for a moment, like he was genuinely upset, but then added, rather coldly, 'Standard practice for the families of traitors.' He sat down and I was clearly dismissed, but before I left his office he said, 'Leave your pass on the desk.' He was one for detail.

There was not much I needed to pack, just a lipstick from my drawer and a photograph of my mother in a frame, which I kept on my desk. Dressed, but before leaving, I looked around the comfortable room, with its sofa and chairs that visitors would nervously recline in before being summoned in to see the Academician. I had always liked the room. Only, I would not miss the beady eye of Lenin looking down from his vantage point on the wall on my every activity and, I have to admit, also my long periods of inactivity. I, somehow, thought of the slogan, *Lenin has died, but his cause lives on.* Then, I recalled my colleague, Varvara Pavlova's quip at our recent after-work party: *Brezhnev has died but his body lives on.* It helped lighten the heaviness for a brief moment.

---

[13] Not officially recognised in the Soviet Union.

I walked down the corridor as uprightly as I could. Turning the corner to the reception I nearly bumped into Varvara. It was her birthday the following day and I had already made her a smart lace collar, which I was looking forward to giving her at the after-work party to be held with a few colleagues. Varvara had access to the spiritus[14] and she was skilled in mixing it with just the right amount of fresh juices to make refreshing but highly intoxicating aperitifs, as we called them, to celebrate special occasions. Now, Varvara looked highly embarrassed, was about to say something but clamped her mouth shut and shot past. Clearly, everyone had been warned not to fraternise with those associated with traitors. Outside, the wind chilled my tears to ice.

I managed to get a seat on the tram and rested my head against the window. Its coldness seemed to sooth me but, at a set of points, the tram rocked and I knocked my head rather violently. It was if Professor Lebedev had punched me and I felt an anger rise. I remembered a strange incident a week before. Professor Lebedev had summoned me into the office and, acting rather strangely, beckoned me over to his desk. He sniffed the air and then asked, 'Do you smell something?' I sniffed.

    'No,' I replied.

    'Are you sure? It doesn't smell of old people does it? Old people have a curious smell.'

---

[14] 100% alcohol.

'No, I can't smell anything like that.' Now I wished I had said, 'Yes, I smell something peculiar. It smells of brevibacterium linens.' Having read the Professor's correspondence, I knew that this bacterium made sweaty feet smell like cheese. The thought cheered me up marginally.

The Professor had always been aloof with me, never using the familiar, but he saved most of his bile for Professor Semenov, Head of Virology. The two of them would posture endlessly and they always made for great talking points at our after-work parties.

I wondered briefly how to pay my boss back for my heartless dismissal and thought I might send a note to his wife saying simply, 'Your suspicions are correct.' She had appeared in the office unexpectedly last month looking rather flustered and emotional. I made an excuse that her husband was at a meeting at the Academy of Science but I should have told the truth - that he was visiting his mistress. *No, I wouldn't do that, however tempting.* I realised. *I would rise above it.*

I never warmed to the Professor but I did like working at the Institute and, as my boss was out of the office a great deal on Institute, Party business or personal business, I had plenty of free time. I sat upright and wondered what would happen to the dahlias and cats at the Institute? When the professor was away, and after the correspondence had been opened and urgent matters dealt with, I had the rest of the day to myself. In the spring I would plant out dahlias in the small garden between the administrative block and the laboratories and throughout the summer I would tend them. By August they were a talking point, and a large bunch of multicoloured flowers always brightened the professor's office until the first frosts.

As for the cats, I had taken responsibility for feeding the stray ones that lived in the cellar of the outbuildings. There was one in particular, Triangle Face I called him, that had become friendly and, whenever I fed them, he would brush against my legs. The others stayed true to their alley cat status and kept a watchful distance.

I also thought about one of my admirers, Professor Petrov. He would, on the most minor of matters, come to my boss's office whenever he was away. I knew it was just to see me and to pass a while in conversation. Whilst it was nice that he wanted to see me, the sad fact was that he was totally boring and I soon had to find urgent jobs to attend to. As a widower, and a painfully shy man, his work had become his whole life and it was the only thing he had to talk about. He would tell me of the projects he was working on as if everyone would be interested in the fine detail.

One of the projects I remembered the Professor telling me about involved finding out how much horse manure it would take to keep a greenhouse ice free through the winter. Unfortunately, the answer had been that the greenhouse, whatever size, would have to be stacked almost to the roof with horse manure. He was another of the many characters who we made fun of in our gatherings.

I thought about the termination of my pay at Christmas. *We always have duck on the 24th; now it is clear that economies are needed. This year it will have to be pork.* I was even pleased that, after such a terrible shock of being dragged to the Big House earlier, I could now be so practical. I even started to think of other budgeting.

With my salary and Svetlana's pension we had a reasonable income, enough anyway to buy some treats when they were available. After all the expenses, including the cost of heating in winter, I had managed to save a small amount but I knew that this would have to cover Svetlana's funeral expenses. *Who else would pay? Sonja?* Her daughter had virtually no savings after spending on Pappa's care and buying Pappa's grandchildren essentials like shoes and books. *But what was there to do? I will have to dip into my savings. Jobs are not easy to find and, God forbid, maybe even references are not forthcoming from the Institute?*

The possibility of not being employed again didn't bear thinking about, but I immediately started to think about it and how I might make a living. *I have skills. I am good at drawing, although there is no money in that. I am also good at sewing and easily make nice things like the lace collar I was going to give Varvara.* In my spare time, I made pretty bordered scarves and I turned cheap, massed produced items like gloves into desirable objects with embroidered patterns and frilly edges.

My spirits rose then fell. *Where to sell them?* I didn't want to rent a stall in an open market and sell in all weathers trying to attract customers from such a poor crowd. I decided to put the question of employment to one side, unless it dragged me down. Although I had not experienced a period of melancholia or panic since arriving in Leningrad, I knew the signs to look out for and negative thinking, especially of the catastrophic kind, was one of them.

I got off one stop before my normal one, as on the way back there was a corner shop that normally sold reasonably edible meat and I decided that a proper meal was called for. Not a celebration of course, but some comfort was needed after such a terrible day. Luckily the queue was small, although, when I got the counter, I was disappointed to see that the selection was limited to a choice between blue-looking chickens, herrings that I knew would be bitter, or some made-in-Latvia sausage. Whenever I saw the shelves so empty I could not help but think of the old joke of the man who walks into the butchers and asks for fish[15]. Despite the events of the day, I still smiled.

I took a blue chicken[16] together with some vegetables and paid the cashier one-rouble sixty kopeks before deciding to buy a bottle of Agdam[17], which I felt would help me sleep at night.

---

[15] The joke referred to did not need to be fully explained as everyone knew it. A man walks into a shop where the shelves and counter are completely empty. He asks for fish and the shopkeeper says, 'This is a butchers, we don't have meat. Over the road is the fishmonger; there they don't have fish.

[16] It is a common recollection from Soviet times that chickens were of a bluish colour, probably due to being washed in chlorine and frozen.

[17] A type of fortified wine.

2.30pm

By the time I reached my block it was only two-thirty but virtually dark. Car headlights illuminated the ice crystals swirling in the air and old snow on the road, like porridge, muffled the sound of tyres on the cobbles. What was usually a noisy street had an eerie quality to it.

On opening the door to our rooms, I was greeted with, 'Misha, is that you.' I looked into Svetlana's room.

'No, it's me. I have bought us a nice chicken and will make a stew later on.'

'Don't worry about me, I have been out with Mrs. Volkova and we had afternoon tea.' Svetlana lived in an untroubled fantasy and for that, at least, I had to be thankful. After hanging up my coat, I put the food in the larder next to Mrs Koslova's pickled gherkins, but before doing anything else I needed a sit down. The radiators felt hotter than ever and I had to open the window in the stifling room to let some heat out and yes, also the smell of brevibacterium linens. I smiled.

Before sitting down, I took the sepia photo of my mother out of my bag and studied it - although I knew it very well. It showed her dressed up in a full skirt and embroidered top and she wore a small summer hat. Very beautiful and very Russian. I saw no likeness of myself in her. It seems that my looks had come entirely from the Finnish side of the family.

I had a very small shelf cluttered with favoured souvenirs and pictures and I was about to place the photo of my mother next to one of my father together with his new wife, Sonja, on their wedding day but changed my mind and put it next to one of Pavel, which had been taken at the dress rehearsal of *Romeo and Juliet* at the Kirov.

I saw the official photographer take the picture of Pavel and asked him if he wouldn't mind giving me a copy when developed. He replied, 'How could I refuse a request from such a pretty lady – and one with such a slim waist.' He had quite a reputation as a ladies' man and, when I went to his studio, he even tried to take my hand as if to lead me to his dark room. I made a joke and somehow evaded his advances whilst still obtaining a copy of the photo. In a way, I was quite flattered as I was at least twenty years older than him.

On sitting down, I immediately felt like I would never be able to get up again. I remembered the sense of fatigue I experienced after Pavel's birth. A fatigue that didn't emanate from the body but from mental exhaustion. I didn't want to think about that. I told myself I had every right to feel tired and, in any case, I knew that I had an appetite and would, later, be able to get up, prepare the food and eat something.

After the birth of Pavel I lost my appetite completely and had to force food down without any enjoyment. I even lost my appetite for breath. No, I would not think of those days and let my thoughts return to my mother. Placing her photo next to other family members had brought back memories.

For some reason, I remembered getting into bed with Mamma and Pappa when I was very young. They sometimes let me join them at night especially as I used to wake up screaming, which disturbed my sisters. How warm, cosy and safe I felt snuggled up in the middle. My sisters didn't seem to mind this special attention. Maybe my screams frightened them and they were pleased to have me out of the room.

I remembered the Christmas when I was six; the huge ham with swede and carrot mash, the pastry stars filled with prune puree and the rice pudding with cinnamon and fruits, the decorations, candles, the holly and all the presents. All in our best clothes and Mamma looking so happy, so radiant in her late pregnancy.

I also remembered getting into bed with Pappa and crying night after night, this time with my sisters as well under the covers. I remembered asking Pappa, 'Why did God take Mamma?' His answer of, 'Because she is an angel and He wanted her in Heaven,' struck me like a donkey's kick. It was when I turned against God, and even hated Him at that moment, but I didn't say anything.

When the new baby came home, Pappa decided to call her Kristiina. He said that it would help to remind us that God is loving and had given us his only son. I didn't hate Kristiina but I could never love her like my other sisters. After all, it was due to her that Mamma died of septicaemia.

These recollections were not doing me any good at all. I hauled myself out of my comfy chair and headed to the kitchen to make a cup of tea. From the smell of frying onions and garlic I knew that one of my neighbours, Mrs Kuznetsova, was already there. Although her husband was painfully thin, and always looked pale even in summer, he had an unquestionable faith in the health-giving properties of garlic and demanded all his meals be prepared with copious quantities. The smell of the cooking was not unpleasant. What is unpleasant is the smell of garlic once it has been chopped, cooked, ingested, digested and exuded from human pores. You had to keep a safe distance from the Kuznetsovs.

Apart from the odour, Mrs Kuznetsova was pleasant enough and was not a busybody who would trouble me with questions about early morning callers. I was thankful for that. She simply commented, 'You are back early from work.' I could have told her of my day but didn't feel up to that so I said that Svetlana had not been well in the night and had needed looking after. She suggested that eating a raw clove of garlic helped most things and, after tipping the fried garlic and onion into a pot of simmering vegetables, left the kitchen.

I lit one of the gas rings on the small burners on the kitchen surface[18], boiled a kettle and tipped some water into a pot with lime-blossom collected before mid-summer from near Lake Ladoga. I had taken the train to the lakeside with the intention of walking to the village where I was born, but, although it was close, I didn't have the courage to make it there. I knew it would be completely different and, in the end, wanted to hang onto the memories I had. After a few minutes, I tipped the brew into two cups and returned to my rooms. Svetlana was happy to have a cup even though she had just had afternoon tea!

Sitting back down, the lime-blossom tea seemed to act like some Proustian madeleine, as images of our old house came flooding back and I took a mental stroll around it and through its rooms. It was a single story, wood tiled house with a closed veranda that caught even the lowest of winter sun. It was painted, unusually for our village, in a Swedish yellow rather than the normal dark reddish-brown. As you entered the house through the front door you went straight

---

[18] In addition to the main stove in communal kitchens, small burners were supplied to cater for the number of residents wishing to cook.

into the kitchen, which was always wonderfully warm with the log-burning kitchen range constantly lit. From the kitchen you could go through one door to the dining room or through another to the sitting room and then onto our bedrooms. Mamma and Pappa had one, but the largest was filled with five beds for us girls.

Outside, there was a large garden with apple trees and rows of currants and raspberry bushes. Between two of the trees a hammock was strung in the summer. Father had a busy job as a doctor but, when he had the opportunity, he liked to swing in this and there were always one or two of us with him. He put the limit on two 'passengers' as once he had been tipped out with three on board.

Such summers, so light and so long! Then it all changed. Mamma's death changed Pappa and it changed me. I understand now my reaction was a warning sign of what was to come later in my life. I felt empty, drained and didn't want to do anything. I lost interest in studying although I had learnt to read very early and had loved books. I lost interest in school and any outside activities.

Pappa was worried about me, my sisters seemed to cope better, but he was very busy and had a house and large family to look after. Sundays were still taken up with church but were supplemented by a visit to Mamma's grave. What could he do? He had some help from a local woman who was efficient rather than maternal and fortunately, Asta, my oldest sister was old enough to cook and look after us until father got home late and tired from the hospital.

When the Russians came and piled us Finns into Stolypin trains[19], I was not, misguidedly, that upset. Only, I cried because we left without Asta, my eldest sister, who had gone with our grandparents to visit friends in Helsinki and had become stranded on the Red Army's invasion[20]. Apart from that, I welcomed

---

[19] During the Stolypin reform in Russia, which led to massive resettlement of peasants and prisoners in Siberia, a special type of carriage was introduced for these settlers. It consisted of two parts: a standard passenger compartment for a peasant and his family and a large zone for their livestock and agricultural tools. After the Bolshevik Revolution, the authorities found these carriages convenient for transport of larger numbers of incarcerated convicts and exiles. The guards used the passenger compartments and the convicts and exiles were transported in the carriages once used for livestock.

[20] The Soviet's invaded Finland on 30th November 1939, three months after the outbreak of World War II. This was the start of what was subsequently called the Winter War, which ended three and a half months later with the Moscow Peace Treaty on 13th

the change; the chance to get away from the house and the constant reminder of Mamma's absence. I used to go to the kitchen expecting every time to see her there or hear her tinkling laugh from the garden.

When we were herded away, I thought that it was the beginning of an adventure, or at least a new beginning. I didn't know that by hardening my heart to God I had doomed Pappa to a life of penury. How I remember those first years. Pappa worked seven days a week boiling up trees in huge vats and came home exhausted, hungry and reeking of tar and turpentine.

I understood that my thinking was moving into dangerous territory. I had to keep busy rather than letting sad thoughts drift in and sitting in these gloomy rooms was not helping. I sat up quickly realising that I had a job to do. I had to let Sonja and my sisters know about what had happened to Pavel. *But what had happened to him? He had no money on which to live in London. Who was looking after him?* I realised that I best not start worrying about these thoughts and needed to busy myself. Sonja did not have a telephone but I had the number of Kristiina's work place and maybe, in an emergency, I could telephone there?

_____

March 1940.

3.00pm

I had just got up to look for Kristiina's number when I heard the telephone ring in the hallway below. The unofficial answerer, Mrs. Morozova, shouted up the stairway in an irritated voice, 'Comrade Mednis, a call.' Mrs. Morozova was a nasty, spiteful woman who loved her role as telephone answerer and, with her door slightly ajar, could eavesdrop on all conversations. I went downstairs, lifted the heavy receiver off the top of the apparatus and said, 'Hello.'

'Hilkka?'

'Sonja!' I was surprised to hear from her and, after she paused, I suddenly thought that the KGB must have visited her. She must already know of Pavel's defection.

'Hilkka, I have very sad news. Your father passed away this morning.'

'Oh...'

'I am sorry... In the end it was very quick, very peaceful. I would have told you to come but... Of course, he was very ill. We should count our blessings I suppose.' Sonja's voice was low and I could tell that she had been crying. I didn't know whether it was because I was already reeling from the events of the day but I didn't feel anything.

'Yes, will you let me know when the funeral is?' was all I could say.

'Of course.'

'And how are Lotta, Ilona and Kristiina?'

'Your sisters are all well and with me here. Do you want a word?' I hesitated, 'Hilkka, are you there?'

'Yes... but no, not now thank you. Please pass on my love. I will come to the funeral and we can speak then.'

'How is Mama?'

'She is completely in her own world, but contented I think.'

'Now I will be able to come and look after her. You have been doing it for too long, you need a rest.'

'Thank you. Let's talk about that when I see you.'

'I will call back soon with the details. By the way, I called you first at the Institute. They said that you weren't available.'

'No, I had a day off... Christmas shopping.'

'Lots of love.'

'To you too.'

It felt like I would have intruded on my family's grief to let them know about Pavel, but I knew that I would have to telephone Kristiina the following day to impart the news. As I walked up the stairs I thought, *This is too much; this is turning into the worst day of my life.* Then I reflected on the glib reaction and immediately knew that this was not the case. Nothing could compare to that day. The day I was one step away from killing myself.

I told Svetlana that my father had died. She said,

'Sorry to hear that.' For a moment, I thought that she might have remembered him, my father and her daughter's husband, but it was not to be, as she added, 'Please pass on my condolences to your mother.'

I sat in my room waiting for the tears to come but they did not. I didn't feel anything different. *Was it the effects of the day or just that I had expected the news?* But expecting the death of a loved one does not take away from the grief of their passing. I understood that once the effects of the day wore off I would begin to feel great sadness for the loss of Pappa for he was a great man. In truth, I had thought of his passing over recent months and had begun to rehearse the eulogy I planned to say at his graveside or wake.

Pappa, what a great loss our family has suffered with your passing. You have been our constant source of comfort in hard times and you have been with us in our joyous moments. You have guided and inspired. You never complained or were bitter or angry at what Soviet life threw at you (although we were bitter and angry on your behalf). You were unquestioning in your faith and belief that these trials and tribulations were inconsequential, as, one day, our suffering would be over and we would be with Jesus. Now you are at peace with Him (Oh, I do hope you are even though I cannot believe that I will be joining you).

Do you remember those words you said to Janis and me on our wedding day? I do, for they are engraved on my heart. When we have hope that daylight will replace the dark skies; when we have hope that the sun will banish the ice and when we have hope that new life will rise from the once frozen ground, we can live positively. But hope is not enough to live life to the full. Hope must be accompanied by love. You lived your life in hope and love. You gave us hope in the dark hours and your love was constant and unquestioning.

You were a caring doctor, hardworking member of Project 503[21] and administrator on Russia's great railways but most of all you were an extraordinary

---

[21] Stalin's massive Trans-Polar Railway Project to connect Vorkuta through Yermakova and on past Norilsk with the final destination being the Bering Straits. The railway was so secret that the prisoners used to construct it were not told where they were taken. The project needed cheap labour and every seven to ten kilometres along the route were prison camps with 1500 to 2000 prisoners in each and around 200 guards. The equipment was basic; crowbars, shovels, wheelbarrows and spades. Men stood shoulder to shoulder like the pyramid builders of ancient Egypt. Untold numbers died on the construction and when the project was finally stopped after Stalin's death the railway quickly sank into the permafrost.

son, father and husband. You have departed to a better world but your presence remains; carried with us in our hearts.

I knew that most of what I wanted to say would have to be amended; certainly references to hard times under the Soviets, Jesus and heaven and perhaps even Project 503 was still secret, but, in saying the eulogy to myself, it provided some comfort.

I pondered on the nature of the funeral. *If only it could be in the church near our old village bordering Lake Ladago and for Pappa to be buried next to Mamma.* I had already taken some solace from the thought that we could scatter his ashes in what was once Finland. In thinking of my eulogy, I smiled and wondered, *As Pappa is reunited with Mamma in heaven, what will happen with Sonja when she joins them? Pappa had enough love in him for two women; he deserved the attention of both his wives looking after him. That is heaven for you!*

Christmas shopping! What a thing to say to Sonja. And what to buy and for whom? Svetlana doesn't need anything and I had just treated myself to some wool to knit a pair of gloves from. Christmas... I was becoming sleepy and my mind wandered. *What is Christmas really? A slight rise in cadence between one day and the next.*

I wondered how was Pappa able to cope all those

years without a proper celebration of Jesus' birth? I don't know how he survived many things; the hardship, lack of food, mind-numbing monotony at work and the separation from his church. There were plenty of Old Believers[22] and Orthodox Christians[23] but very few Lutherans. He must have decided early on he was going to be his own church as he never sought out people to pray or read the scriptures with. Would I, in his position, have kept my faith? Clearly not; mine was lost at the first hurdle. Well, if not completely lost, changed for the worse. But, would it have helped in my darkest times? It seems that God is loath to intervene in the affairs of man. I doubt very much whether he would have entered my insignificant world, however hard I'd prayed, to darn a hole that surely must have appeared in the fabric of my mind.

How sleepy I felt but was too tired to get up to let more fresh air into the room. Then, before I could prevent the border being crossed, I was asleep.

---

[22] In Eastern Orthodox Church history, the Old Believers or Old Ritualists are Eastern Orthodox Christians who maintain the liturgical and ritual practices as they existed prior to the reforms of Patriarch Nikon of Moscow between 1652 and 1666.
[23] Russian Orthodox Christians.

3.50pm

I awoke with a jolt and could not immediately place myself. Then, thinking that I was in Moscow's Number One Hospital, my heart started to bang against my chest. Thankfully, it was just momentary and I realised, with relief, I was in a small, dark, stuffy room in Leningrad. However, the initial thought had been so powerful I couldn't help but recall the time I had first woken in that hospital with a strange sensation, a pulsing and flickering, like a butterfly was inside my head. The nurses were all around me evidently pleased to see me released from what they said was a long coma.

I remember clearly what had happened before I found myself in the hospital. Janis and I were on our way back from Riga to Siberia having agreed to go into voluntary exile. By chance, we were in Moscow at the time of Stalin's funeral and we got caught up in the huge crowd that had come to pay their respects (or possibly just make sure he was dead). The last memory was of myself screaming, 'Jani, Jani,' as the great suffocating crowd prised our hands apart.

When I was informed, with medical brutality, that my husband had suffocated and I was pregnant, the butterflies swarmed and then turned into bats and their wings beat so violently that they caused sparks and the sparks set light to the dry tinder of my

49

thoughts and, before I could douse the flame, my head was on fire. I actually felt the intense heat, heard the crackling and smelt the burning. It was so real, so visceral, I was only surprised that no one could see the flames.

I was given a sleeping pill that night but it gave no respite from the all-consuming flames that rampaged unrelentingly for days. As I was on fire, I desired self-immolation, to cease to be.

Eventually, I just wanted to escape my seared mind where thoughts smoked like embers on a charred forest floor. Should one person have felt so much pain? If I felt hope, it was simply to be empty; that is, free of pain and ultimately – oblivion.

Thankfully, nothing lasts forever. Tornados blow themselves out, fires run out of fuel, tides turn and eventually the searing pain receded and I sat amongst the smoking remains of the vast taiga[24]. The taiga became green but this was not the rebirth of hope.

I was as if I were sitting in the vastness of the taiga in a permanent damp mist and there was incessant

———————————————

[24] Also known as boreal forest or snow forest, the taiga is a vast ecosystem characterised by coniferous forests consisting mostly of pines, spruces and larches.

dripping and only the silence of the absorbing, mossy forest carpet. This was no romantic notion. The taiga was not external to me. I was the taiga and bizarrely, at the same time, I was in the taiga. Its vast expanse filled my head and it absorbed my being. And, just as there is in the taiga, there were real dangers. I could not sit for fear of being eaten by unnamed and unknown predators and movement brought fears of being sucked into a kind of swamp. I craved moments of release from the taiga but it never came. I could not think of the future and the past was inaccessible. Even the wish to think of it, to release me from the horrible present moment brought on a tightening of my chest. I concentrated on being someone else whilst experiencing strange disconnected sensations that easily became one of falling.

I just wanted to feel normal. I just wanted to feel normal grief and maybe normal hope for a new life. However, the taiga consumed me and I feared that I would slip permanently into a state of madness or that I was a schizophrenic and would be locked in a padded cell.

The doctors came and asked questions. Although my head whirled and my thoughts were racetrack fast, I found it hard to move quickly and my answers took time to form. I was told that I was melancholic, which was natural they informed me after the shock of losing my husband in the great crush of visitors to

Stalin's grave.

I looked up to the dark paintings on the wall of my room in Leningrad and they seemed to press in on me. I knew that this introspection and reminiscence was not good at all. I felt selfish. If I was to think of anyone it should be Pappa or Pavel. However, just by bringing his name to mind, my thoughts were off again.

Pavel, what a mother I have been. It is amazing that you have grown into a caring and talented man. It had nothing to do with his mother's early nurturing – or lack of it. At first, I didn't want my baby son near to me, let alone to wean him. I tried to move my thoughts on but, somehow, they kept returning to when I was pregnant and the early years of motherhood.

The taiga stretched on in time and space and continued whilst I was discharged and sent to a nearby hostel. It also stretched out before me on the train that bore me home to Siberia, to my waiting father, his wife, Sonja and my three sisters. I cannot recall the hugs that must have been exchanged or the sadness on Sonja's face to be without her son. The taiga sucked all feelings out of me except for fear and dread, and these continued even after the birth of Pavel. Thank goodness for my sisters. They had all moved to Kanska, Siberia when Pappa got a job there and they took it upon themselves to care for my

52

baby.

I was closeted in a tiny room in Kristiina's Stalin block[25] apartment and this small space became my sanctuary. My world shrank from the whole of the Soviet Union, to the taiga, to the room and then to the bed. I slept and sat in it and was loath to leave. I was also loath to talk to even my sisters. Thankfully they were not chatterboxes. It was one of the characteristics of our family; words were taken seriously and we tended to avoid unnecessary small talk. I remember Pappa saying, 'Take a man by his words and a bull by its horns.' When I reluctantly left the room to visit the toilet, I felt the difference between inside and outside as Pavel might have experienced between being in my womb and the world.

Pappa, Sonja and my other sisters were constant visitors. Sisters encouraged me to get fresh air or do something, anything, I think they were becoming frustrated with my self-imposed isolation. Father sat with me in the gloom, held my hand and would occasionally say something in Finnish. Hearing the language of my childhood soothed me. It must have been the spring of 1955 when he asked whether I wanted to accompany him to the market to buy some vegetables.

---

[25] Apartment blocks built in the Stalin era. These were well built with large rooms and high ceilings.

I had felt slightly less fearful in the preceding weeks and summoned up the courage to go with him to the market. We put on our winter coats; spring in Siberia still has a raw wind to it, and headed through the front door and into the stairwell. The brightness was startling and nearly overpowered me. I had been living in a shell, which was now removed and I felt exposed. My mind was lacerated but I wanted to get out.

Outside, the Stalin blocks looked like they had sunk into the winter mud and grey apparitions walked past, heads down to avoid eye contact and to watch out for potholes obscured by sludgy water. Pappa held my hand as we went to the market but, as we neared it, the increase in the number of people made me feel like they were pressing on me and I had difficulty in breathing. I felt short of breath and floaty but Pappa squeezed my hand gently, which gave me the courage to carry on. In my head I just repeated, you can do this, one step at a time. Before I had time to panic, Pappa had bought a kilo of old-looking potatoes and a large woman in a thick coat with a fur-lined hood handed these to him. Her hands looked as red raw as my mind felt.

I remember Pappa saying before he left that afternoon, 'The way is never through yourself.' I thought that he was going to add that the way is through Jesus Christ but he did not. Instead he added in Finnish, 'ei tule etsien, vaan eläen' –

happiness is not found in searching but by living. I understood he was advising, be outside of myself and experience movement and things that were not just in my head. He understood.

Thankfully, I began to improve and started to take an interest in Pavel, but even later I was prone to panic. There was the time when Kristiina was late bringing Pavel home from a ride in his carriage. I knew they were both dead, killed in a terrible accident. I pictured the pram as twisted metal and it was so clear, it could not have been anything but real. When they arrived home, safe and sound, it was if they had risen from the dead. And the first time I ventured out alone I felt that a rising anxiety might spill over into pure panic and I would be forever-after a prisoner in my sister's small room.

There were bad days but improvement was slow and steady. I patted my knee in self-congratulation and remembered also that drawing had been so helpful in my recovery, especially after the ordeal in Riga. Riga; what a terrible time that was. But, I wasn't going to think about that now.

4.15pm

In the kitchen two neighbours were cooking and chatting. Mrs. Stepanova was frying mushrooms and Mrs. Koslova was putting a tray of potatoes to roast in the oven. Both acknowledged my presence with a, 'Good evening,' resumed their animated conversations and went back to their cooking. I smiled a small, ironic smile as both activities reminded me of my worst times in Riga. It seemed that, somehow, I was being compelled to remember my experiences there.

Unbeknownst to my husband, Janis, I had seriously contemplated ending my miserable life and the cooking reminded me of two methods I had considered; mushroom poisoning and putting my head in the gas oven. Only, I had decided I didn't know enough about mushrooms to be sure they would kill me – rather than simply making me sick – and ovens always reminded me of a funny incident involving my eldest sister, Asta. I understood that levity and suicide were incompatible so both mushrooms and ovens were removed as potential means of escape.

Asta, as the oldest sister, was the first to be asked out on a date by a local boy. She was terribly excited and took forever to get ready. Then she decided, at the last minute, to wash her hair, but, as it was thick and long, it took quite a while to dry. With the time of the date fast approaching, Asta had the idea to put her head into the warm oven to dry her hair. Unfortunately, it was hotter than she had anticipated and we all heard the screams as she ran to our room, her hair badly singed and frazzled. The smell of burning hair hung around the kitchen for a long time after.

I have never been good at small talk and, as a result, was rarely brought into kitchen conversations. Now, I was happier than ever not to participate. However, as I plucked the remaining feathers from the blue chicken, and singed the hard-to-remove ones over the stove, the chatter of the ladies took my mind off my own troubles. 'Did you hear about Mrs. Nikolayeva's resurrected carp?' Mrs Stepanova enquired.

'No.'

'Well, let me tell you. She bought a frozen carp from the market and put it in the sink full of warm water to thaw overnight. In the middle of the night Mrs. Vershinina heard a flapping sound coming from the kitchen and found the carp had come alive and was splashing about.'

'I have heard of that happening.'

'She woke Mrs. Nikolayeva who acted like some sort of miracle had taken place. Mrs Vershinina was all for giving the carp a good thwack on the head, but Mrs. Nikolayeva would have none of it and said something like, no it is a sign that it must live.'

'Oh dear, what did they do with it?'

'Mrs. Nikolayeva picked up the fish and took it to a filled bath. Then they went back to bed.'

'Is the carp still there?'

'No. When Mrs. Nikolayeva got up to tend the fish, it had gone, disappeared!

'I've never heard of a resurrected carp vanishing before.'

'I think it's a mystery easily solved. Mr. Orlov was found drunk on the stairs. He was clutching a bottle of vodka, worth just about what you would pay for a fresh carp at the all-night pub.'

Having cut up the chicken and vegetables I put them into a big pot on the stove with some seasoning. Mrs. Stepanova and Mrs. Koslova had stopped cooking but were enjoying the opportunity to gossip. 'Mr. and Mrs. Baginsky have been refused exit visas.' Mrs. Stepanova announced.

'Pity! But I thought all Jews could leave whenever they want.' Anti-Semitism seeped from Mrs. Koslova as easily as honey from a cut comb.

'It's probably the old joke...You know the one where the Jew asks the KGB officer why he has been refused an exit visa.'

'I remember.' Mrs. Koslova smiled but Mrs. Stepanova finished the ending in any case.

'Yes, he is informed that he has state secrets. The Jew is surprised and says, 'but I work in a factory that is ten years behind everywhere else.' The KGB man says, 'that is the secret'.' Both of them chuckled again at the old joke and then looked at me in some embarrassment. I am sure that they were desperate to know why I had been hauled off to the Big House, but did not ask.

The chicken stew would need to simmer for a few hours to tenderise the tough meat and I felt that I needed to get out of our rooms. Although the weather was miserable, I wanted to walk, move and distract myself, rather than sit and ponder. I decided that it would be a good idea to visit Pavel's hostel and maybe take some of his clothes and the bear if he wasn't going to occupy the room for some while. I didn't want to think of him not ever returning.

I dressed warmly and ventured into the street, which was now busy at the end of the working day with people walking home as quickly as they could. I always enjoyed walking to Pavel's hostel as it took me past the Vaganova Academy and its columns created the illusion of dancing figures. Maybe it was just the association with the Kirov or maybe the architect had this effect in mind when he designed the beautiful building.

I am a quick walker and came to the hostel in a short time. The main door was always slightly ajar and a babushka sat wrapped up in the entrance making sure that only students, Kirov dancers and known associates were allowed in. She recognised me and let me up the stairs without question. From the kitchen on Pavel's floor there was the sound of young people laughing and a voice said, 'His port de bras! What a joke.'

I didn't look into the kitchen although I would undoubtedly have known a few of the people there but went on down the corridor to Pavel's room. When I turned the corner, I was shocked to see his door had been taped and a seal set over it, as if this was some crime scene. I couldn't help but take a sharp breath and had to lean against the wall for a few seconds to steady myself.

Gathering myself, I went back down the corridor and opened the kitchen door. The faces of the young people turned to look at who was entering. One of them, a friend of Pavel's named Antonina, I immediately recognised and she beckoned me in with, 'Come on in. I am sorry... It must be difficult.'

'Yes.' I replied but really didn't know what to say. 'I'm sorry, I've disturbed you. I just came to see if there was anything of Pavel's that I needed to look after, but I see they have sealed his room.'

'Yes. They came early this morning.' Antonina confirmed, 'I don't think they have taken anything away, so I am sure you'll be able to have his things in time... Have you heard from Pavel?' I didn't answer straight away. 'Sorry, I didn't mean to pry.' Antonina added.

'No. No, it's fine. Only, it is a big surprise to me. I haven't heard from him and don't know why he left, but somehow I don't think he will be coming back... do you?'

One of the young men offered me a seat at an oilcloth-covered, tea-stained table covered with chipped mugs. I was pleased to be treated with such courtesy, as I felt the need to sit down. My legs were a little shaky. I took off my hat, scarf and coat and was glad to rest for a short while. Then, I was given a mug of hot tea. One of the other men, whom I didn't recognise said, 'It's not unusual you know.' I was unsure as to what he meant.

'To defect?' I asked.

'For blues[26], yes.'

'I thought it might be something to do with their relationship but did you know in advance?'

'No. I am sure that they didn't plan it but when they tasted the freedom on offer it must have been very appealing to stay.'

'Is there such freedom?' He surely could tell from my voice that I was sceptical.

'I can only guess at that, but I know what they face here. Pavel and Oleg are in love and yet they were frightened to go out in Leningrad. Here, in the house is fine, we are all very accommodating, but outside is a tough world.'

The man looked across the table to a tall young man with cropped hair and distinct cheekbones. 'Only last

---

[26] Soviet slang for homosexuals.

week, Dmitri and I had to run for our lives when some gang decided that they'd enjoy beating us to a pulp. We weren't holding hands or anything but they have a nose that sniffs out the blues. If I had been picked to go to London, I would definitely not be on the plane home.'

The young people were good-hearted and generous even though I guessed they risked some sanction if found associating with the mother of a traitor. As they talked about some of the problems of being homosexual in Russia, I thought back over Pavel's childhood.

I remember Pavel had liked girls. Maybe, on reflection, he was too comfortable in their company. As a young boy and teenager he had had his favourites whom he liked to sit next to in class. I had no idea he was attracted to other boys. Probably he wasn't. Maybe it was only when he went to the Vaganova.

I looked around the table at the faces of the good-looking young men. At the Vaganova he would have seen the most beautiful of male bodies. Surely the young body of the male dancer is more alluring with their strong thighs, distinct buttocks and flat stomachs compared to the reedy, underfed-looking and flat-chested female counterparts?

When the subject had been thoroughly aired, I asked.

'Did Professor Nikolyukin get a grilling?'

'Certainly.' A swan-necked girl replied. 'After the KGB had interviewed him for hours, he addressed his students.' She mimicked the Professor's rather lofty speech. 'London is a city of decadence whose rottenness would only corrupt them. They will lose their dancing technique and moral integrity. They are classical dancers but will be tempted into modern dance. The West will take their youth, use them and spit them out. They have only one thing left for them, to come home immediately. No one here can understand their action.' She then looked a little embarrassed as if she had been insensitive and added, 'But everyone knew that he was forced to say this by the KGB.'

6.15pm

I left the hostel wishing I hadn't gone there. It was clear that Pavel was being treated as a serious criminal and if he came home he would surely be put in prison rather than reemployed at the Kirov. I felt the beginning of what I anticipated was a chasm of loss and bereavement.

I understood that, for the rest of the day, to protect myself from collapsing, I must focus on what was around me. After taking my leave from Pavel's fellow lodgers, I decided to walk a while around the city and was pleased that the wind had abated and the bright upturned bowl of the moon was tipping its silvery contents onto the frost-covered path. When a passing cloud obscured it, I remembered that I had to look at my thoughts as clouds in the sky; look at them, observe, but try not to follow them.

As I turned into Ostrovskogo Square I noticed bright lights and a big lorry with Lenfilm[27] painted on its side. Clearly, scenes were being shot for a film. I thought it would be interesting to have a look and see if I recognised any of the actors but, as I

---

[27] Located in Leningrad, Kinostudiya Lenfilm was the production unit of the Cinema of the Soviet Union, with its own film studio.

65

approached the set, I was told that I couldn't pass. With only the bright lights to look at in the distance, I decided to skirt around the filming and continue on my way – to where, I had no idea.

Just past the cordon, there were two beer stands and a vodka window. People were jammed up near the counter with the queue thinning out further away. As I walked past I was surprised and amused to see the Tsar and Kaiser towards the back of the throng. Tall and elegantly dressed in a long coat with fur collar, the Tsar, with his moustache and pointed beard, was chatting to the Kaiser who wore his, tell-tale, pickelhaube.

I decided to walk by to take a closer look and, when I approached, I saw that the Tsar was the actor, Alexander Alkohov. He wasn't a huge star but I always liked his performances, especially as he was good-looking and delivered jokes with perfect timing.

One of my favourite pastimes was to go to the cinema. For sixty Kopeks I was transported to a world of delight and my favourite film of all had Alkohov in it in a supporting role as a dashing cavalry officer. I decided to pretend I was also queuing for beer and stood a few people back from the Tsar and Kaiser to take in the scene and have a closer look at my matinee idol.

The huddle around the stall largely comprised men

wearing grey coats and clutching an assortment of jars and teapots for their beer. There were only a few women – five or six at most. They were noisier and more impatient. One of them kept insisting, 'Let me go ahead of you, out of respect for a war veteran's widow!' In front of me was a man in a railway workers' uniform. To the left of me stood a ragged individual who wore canvas shoes even though it was below freezing.

The situation was bizarre and funny. Too intent on getting their foaming brew, no one said anything to the Tsar or the Kaiser. As I moved closer to the stand, the people in front became more animated and I just heard a snippet of conversation between the Tsar and the Kaiser. 'What are you taking?' The Tsar asked.

'Vodka'

'Oh, I thought you had switched to white wine.'

'Would be nice, but this is a vodka and beer stall.' Close up, I could see the Tsar was even more handsome in real life. At one point he even turned and looked at me. His eyes seemed to twinkle in the moonlit sky and then I chastised myself for behaving like some love-struck teenager.

Just as we approached the stand there was a clarification as to who was to be served first, and I heard one ragged-looking man explain, 'I'm behind the bald guy. The Tsar's, behind me and you come after the Kaiser.' Having queued for the beverage, I decided to take vodka for inner warmth.

After I had been served, and standing on the foam-flecked pavement, I looked around for the Tsar and Kaiser but they had disappeared. The bizarre incident though had raised my spirits and I decided to go over and sit a while on a bench and try to remember all of the films that Alkohov had been in.

Serious drinkers were also dotted around, oblivious to the cold, and some were sitting together, deep in conversation. The cold slats immediately chilled my backside and the icy vodka scorched my throat. I would get up as soon as anyone else wanted to share the seat.

I initially recalled the old black and white film in which Alkohov played a dashing cavalry officer. However, it wasn't long before my thoughts returned to the events of the day and then to my uncertain future. *What will happen when Sonja comes back to look after Svetlana? I'll have no room and no job.*

The prospect of being homeless reminded me that I had never felt truly at home since leaving Finland and, despite my best attempts at fitting in by learning the language and never trying to stand out as Finnish, I felt an outsider. The vodka had a warming affect and also a nostalgic one. I thought of home in Finland and pictured myself in the sitting room of an evening listening to the chatter of my sisters and the hiss of the paraffin lamps.

I recalled the reds, blues and greens of a rag rug[28] that used to be in the sitting room. It was made of woven strips of recycled fabric and I remembered Grandmother making it on her loom. Pointing to the section in red, she said that this was from one of her mother's old aprons. The bright blue portion was part of Grandpa's old work uniform. The green fabric came from a pair of shorts father wore as a young child. I thought of this old rug as if it was a cherished heirloom, as if it embodied my family history.

Looking back, I understood that I had been a fearful child but everything had been connected and safe, which had comforted me. Now, I was disconnected and unsafe. Soviet life was like walking over a lake in spring; would the ice be strong enough? Each step carried the prospect of falling in the dark water beneath the thinnest veneer. And I had never been brave. I thought about my sisters who had all seemed so much stronger than myself and I returned to a theme that I had always found interesting; that of names.

My oldest sister is Asta and her name means super strength or divine strength. I remembered the time when Pappa set Asta a task of taking us on a night

---

[28] Popular Finnish rug made at home on a loom.

walk. It was a cold, but lovely, moonlit evening. Snow sparkled on the great pine and spruce trees and squeaked underfoot. As we approached a clearing there was the faintest of crackling sounds, and then we could see on the horizon and across the sky shades of orange, red, yellow, green and blue appear like mysterious dancing figures swaying back and forth. It was the Aurora Borealis but Pappa said that this was fox fire and told us that it had been created as an arctic fox ran past the mountains and grazed its fur; which caused sparks to fly into the sky. Later we saw reindeers in the distance grazing on lichens and leaves.

The walk had been magical but when we turned to go back home Asta began to feel uneasy. In the darkness, she had mistakenly taken the wrong route. With the snow covering any clear paths, and the appearance of clouds obscuring the night sky, she wanted Pappa to help get them back, but he refused and encouraged her to carry on. Asta, at first, was very worried but then settled down and made the right choices to get us home. When we got home Pappa gave Asta a hug and said, 'Well done. I wanted you to learn that we need to finish what we start regardless of how hard the task is at hand.'

This was one of the small lessons in resilience and perseverance that Pappa used to teach my sisters. Only, I felt that I'd not properly learnt the lessons as I didn't feel that I had my sisters' mental toughness or *sisu* in Finnish. I knew that if Pappa had put me in Asta's position I would have collapsed under the pressure. He never did test me in the same way. I think he knew who could handle it, and who could not, but I nevertheless felt guilty for my weakness.

The second oldest is Lotta. Her name means free woman. She also is a strong character; strong enough to become a Hippy. She was even arrested in 1971 but that didn't stop her from dressing and travelling to others in the System[29]. That took some courage in the Soviet Union.

Next is Ilona, which means the bright one. She is smart and married well.

The youngest is Kristiina - believer in Christ. Next to Pappa she is the most religious.

Then there is me, Hilkka, meaning hood and often associated with Little Red Riding Hood. Yes, that is

---

[29] While Hippies are most associated with the capitalist West, the movement found its way across the Atlantic and took on a unique form in Leonid Brezhnev's stuffy and increasingly stagnant Soviet Union. Thousands of disaffected young citizens banded together in an underground network of self-identified hippies calling themselves *Sistema*, or 'the system'.

me, always afraid of the big bad wolf.

Did Mamma and Pappa have an idea that the names given to us would suit our personalities so well, or did the names provide our destiny?

I didn't want to think about how little I measured up to Pappa's ideal but I recalled the time when he showed the utmost *sisu*. When Pappa carried Janis after his accident for days through the taiga to eventual safety, it was the ultimate act in the face of adversity; of going beyond what we think our limits might be – whether physical, mental or emotional.

6.45pm

I looked around and thought how easily I could have been taken for an alcoholic sitting close to the beer stall in the freezing conditions. It reminded me that I had gradually come to understand that my condition was a bit like alcoholism. One bad thought led to another and, before I knew what was what, I was immersed in something that takes over your mind and body. I even had associated sweats and palpitations.

Like alcoholics who were trying to live a sober life, big commitments, in my case – always think positive thoughts never worked. It was always one day at a time, and some of the days were bad indeed.

Sitting on the cold bench, I was becoming scared. My thoughts are being sucked towards the abyss - back to the terrible times in Riga. Times I never want to think about again. Surely, they would tip me once again into the vortex of depression.

I remembered when Janis came into my life – saved by the heroic efforts of Pappa who carried him, it seems, half way across Siberia after a dreadful accident. His life hung in the balance and I felt huge compassion towards him as he gradually recovered. There were so few educated boys that I could talk to and Janis was clever. I nursed him as if he was part of our family but we had so little time together and as soon as he could walk he was forced to work again.

When he asked me to marry him, I was overjoyed and I did feel love for him. Yes, it was a special time and I loved his mother and my sisters with all my heart as if we were one big family. I wanted to be a good wife and look after him as Mamma had looked after Pappa, even though our circumstances were completely different.

I thought that when we were married, Janis wouldn't want to return to his old home even though he had been granted the right to return to Latvia. When he left without me, I had to hide my sense of desolation.

When we were reunited in Riga, the conditions in which we lived were as bad as in Siberia, but in the East, at least, we didn't have a drunk for a landlord or his daughter plying her trade to the visiting sailors. I hated the rooms we had, but, as I couldn't work, had to put up with them even though the walls seemed to close in and squeeze the breath from me.

At first, I was pleased to be reunited, but, over time, Janis retreated behind a closed door and would not open up however insistent I was. I knew he had problems at work, but he wouldn't talk and when he woke early and paced the room I understood he was keeping things from me, even if he blamed it on pains from the old wound.

As Janis withdrew, my sense of loneliness became intense. The lonelier I felt, the less able I was able to get out. Loneliness grew like the mould on the disgusting bedroom ceiling, preventing contact even though I craved it. Thankfully, on the very odd occasion, I was able to lose myself in the ballet at the Opera House. In the end, I was saved by the delirium that came with illness. Unable to get out of bed, at least I couldn't kill myself.

When we decided to return to Siberia I was happier than I had been for a long time. Then, I recollected the tenderness of our last day in Moscow. How uplifted we both were; even though off to resume our exile in Siberia.

All of these recollections came flooding back, unwanted and unbidden, At the very moment I was worried I would return to the state I had experienced in Riga, I felt a relief flooding through me. I understood that there was a distance between my past and my reality now. I felt that I could think about those times without reliving the emotion that I had experienced then. I could even consider the question that had often hung, unaddressed at the back of my mind; *could I think of that day? The day I decided to go to a station just outside the city to throw myself under a passing express train.*

Janis had left for work when I sat at our rickety table, took out a pen and wrote a note on the back of an envelope, 'Janis, please forgive me, but I don't have the strength to go on.' I had the same feeling of being squeezed but that day it was if I could only take rabbit breaths and the pressure only built as I took a tram, then a trolleybus to Turaida Station, just outside Riga. I knew that the express trains did not stop there and had gathered sufficient speed for death to be quick.

As I approached, I could feel my whole-body squirm as if snakes had taken it over and, although my mind pulsed and clattered, I thought about the welcoming soft, velvet-black eternity ahead. I took myself to the edge of the platform. When I heard the whistle of the express in the distance, I could hardly stand and feared that I would drop immediately onto the track so that the train had time to brake to a halt. I felt dreadful, but I felt worse when the train had passed.

I felt worse than dead. I didn't want to be alive but found that death frightened me and I hated myself; for I was not even brave enough to end my own misery.

I returned to our rooms. They felt as disgusting as before and I ripped up the envelope.

These were my most painful of memories but, strangely on a bench in the middle of Leningrad, I felt elated. I realised that the taiga had lost its strength and the swamp its power to drag me in. I even turned to a fellow drinker to my right and lifted my vodka glass. 'Za Zdarovje'. He toasted back.

The effects of the large measure of vodka were wearing off and I thought of food. I remembered the chicken stew that was bubbling on the stove and then I wanted: creamy salmon soup accompanied by rye bread and rieska - potato flat bread, dessert of Leipäjuust - a sort of cheese, served with a dollop of cloudberry jam and covered in bilberries and lingonberries.

I was not only hungry, I was also homesick. I had the desperate urge to go to our old village. Maybe our house was still there? With the words of the KGB officer ringing in my ears, 'Don't leave the city,' I decided that was just what I was going to do. *I will take the train to Lake Ladoga and then walk the rest of the way. One of the ladies in the kitchen will make sure the stew is turned off.* I was still thinking practically.

7.05pm

I struggled to stand up. The cold had seeped into my bones and I felt stiff but, rather than returning to the overheated fug of my room, I started to make my way to Finlyandskiy Station[30]. I pushed my gloved hands deep into my pockets and headed to Nevsky Prospect to catch the number 27 trolleybus, hoping that I would get a prized seat by the heater.

Fortunately, I did not have to wait long for the trolleybus, but, once those waiting had forced themselves onto it, it was completely full; sprats in a can could not have felt so squashed. It was, at least, warm even if it smelt of old alcohol, wet wool and a hint of brevibacterium linens.

I looked up to the front of the trolleybus to where the ticket machine was and decided that it was too difficult to get to.[31] As I hadn't seen a ticket inspector

---

30 Major railway station in St. Petersburg handling transport to northern destinations including Helsinki and Vyborg. The station is most famous for having been the location where Vladimir Lenin returned to Russia from exile in Switzerland on 16th April 1917 ahead of the October Revolution.

31 Tickets were obtained by dropping money (official fare was four Kopeks) into a box and turning a

for some time, I decided that I wouldn't push past the sullen looking passengers and, instead, hung on a strap as we bumped and rocked along.

Four rows ahead were three schoolboys sitting cramped on two rear-facing seats and they seemed to be looking at me and giggling. I wondered what it could be that amused them when I realised that they were looking past me, and I turned around to see a drunk slumped to one side who, with the next rock of the trolleybus, was about to fall onto the floor. Then, as he began his descent, a hand came out and steadied him. I immediately recognised his saviour to be the Tsar, Alexander Alkohov, and could not resist smiling at him. He smiled back.

At the next stop, I felt my heart sink as three ticket inspectors got on, one in each doorway, ensuring that no ticketless free rider could escape. The trolleybus didn't move off and I awaited my interrogation, thinking, 'This is far from my day, what else is going to happen?'

When the ticket inspector got to me, I started an exaggerated search in my pockets for a lost ticket and then, to the obvious annoyance of the passengers, I looked into my bag in the same theatrical manner. 'Ticket.' The inspector demanded

---

mechanical wheel. The system was easy to cheat and payment was largely a matter of conscience.

in a weary voice; clearly she had seen this charade of searching for a ticket play out many times before.

I was just about to say that I must have lost it, when I felt something being placed into the palm of my hand, which for a moment was down by my side and I clutched it. When I brought it up, my fist contained a ticket and all I could say was, 'Here it is.' The inspector looked at me suspiciously and then moved on. When the trolleybus restarted, I turned around. Alkohov looked at me and I said, 'Thank you'.

I understood that travelling further risked other unforeseen troubles and I decided that to go to Lake Ladoga was simply out of the question. My bravado must have come from the vodka and I got off at the next stop with the intention of returning to my room. When I had stepped down I was surprised to see that Alkohov had also got off the trolleybus. I turned to him and said, 'Many thanks.'

'Pleasure.' In his coat and fedora hat, and with his beard no longer shaped as that of the Tsar, Alkohov looked urbane and debonair.

'I would never have imagined being saved by the Tsar.'

'I thought that was you in the queue at the beer stall... Vodka or beer, which did you have?'

'Vodka.'

'Good choice.'

'Can I take you for a drink to thank you for your kindness?' I had never ever asked a question like this in my life and was surprised by my own forwardness.

'Such a good idea. Where should we go?'

'I don't know this area. I got off the bus as I changed my mind about where I wanted to go and I'm heading home.'

'I don't know it either.'

'Don't you live around here?'

'No.'

'Why did you get off the bus?'

'Because you did.' I felt myself blush even in the cold night air. Alkohov added, 'Aleksey Alkohov. Pleased to meet you.'

'Oh, I know who you are! Hilkka Mednis. Pleased to meet you too.' I really did feel pleased. In fact, I felt quite giddy.

'It is a busy area, there must be a bar or restaurant around here somewhere.' We turned and headed along the wide pavement, which glistened and Alkohov offered his arm.

I asked myself, *When did I last go for a drink with a man? Did I ever go out with Janis? No. Not once.* However, I could not become too immersed in my thoughts as Aleksey had an easy conversational style. He asked, 'Where were you heading?'

'Oh, I just wanted to be out but hadn't realised the time and needed to get back to look after my mother in-law.'

'Oh, you are married?'

'I was. Janis, my husband, died in the crush

at Stalin's funeral.'

'You went to Stalin's funeral?' Aleksey sounded surprised.

'Not exactly. We were in Moscow when it was on and we just got caught up in the crowd.'

'Sorry to hear that. Have you kids?'

'One. He is a ballet dancer at the Kirov, well...'

'Well?'

'Well, he was until today. I had an early morning visit from the KGB to say that my son has defected. And by the way, you are now associating with the mother of a traitor. Very dangerous.'

'I like to live dangerously.'

'Are you married?' Again, I was surprised by my forwardness. I had a reputation of being shy but in this case, I was enjoying not living up to it.

'I was many years ago now. We divorced.'

On the corner of wide boulevard there was a restaurant with a doorman standing outside. Aleksey said a few words to him and we were let through. I wondered whether the doorman had recognised the actor, as it was supposed to be virtually impossible to walk into a restaurant like this without being known.

Inside, I was surprised by the cosiness of the room. It had large, even oversized wooden chairs but they were arranged so that couples were almost in their own private area. After we had hung up our coats, a waiter showed us to a table covered in a red cloth, lit a candle and asked us what we wanted to drink.

Aleksey turned to me and suggested, 'Vodka?' I nodded. Even in the dimness of the restaurant, Aleksey's conker brown eyes shone like newly opened chestnuts.

Whilst we waited for the vodka to arrive, I asked, 'What is the film you are making?'

'I am not sure this'll be a career-defining one. It's a rather silly story of the Tsar and Kaiser getting together to celebrate George V's birthday. Everything goes wrong and it seems that the two of them are completely incompetent. In fact, they couldn't, between them, pour water from a boot.'

'It sounds like it could be amusing.'

'There are a few funny scenes, which I am in.'

'Of course.'

'But the premise is too thin for a whole film and I think it will show.'

A half bottle of vodka and two iced glasses were brought to the table and, after the waiter had poured two measures and departed, I quietly said as a toast, 'To the Tsar.'

'Indeed, may he have a full life.' Aleksey added, 'Would you like something to eat?'

'Maybe a snack, this vodka will go to my head if not.' Aleksey summoned over the waiter, quickly looked at the menu and ordered, 'Salmon on potato cakes and pickled herring on rye bread.'

Aleksey had taken the seat next to me and, with

some effort to shift the heavy chair, turned it slightly towards me before asking, 'Are there any downsides on being beautiful?'

'Are there any downsides on being charming?'

'Oh yes. Charmers are the very worst sort.'

'I had better watch out in that case.' I felt remarkably at ease in his company.

'I don't suppose you have had a good day if you were visited by the KGB.'

'No, it is a shock to be hauled off to the Big House and then hear that you may never see your son again. I'm still trying to take it in.'

'He was in the Kirov, you say.'

'Yes, they were in London.'

'I am told that the food is terrible there and as for the beer, well, they drink it warm. So, you never know, when he wants some pickled herring and a proper drink he might be back.'

'I will drink to that as well.'

I began to feel light headed but I was not quite sure if it was the vodka or being in the company of this handsome and charming man. Aleksey asked, 'What do you like doing of an evening or weekend?'

'I like going to the cinema. In fact, there is rarely a Saturday afternoon that I don't go to the Splendid Palace. I also go to the ballet – at least I did and the rest of the time I look after my mother-in-law. I don't have your exciting life.'

'It's not all beer and sausages.'

'What's it like to be a famous actor?'

'Famous! Who's being charming now?'

'Well, what's it like being an actor?'

'You really want to know?'

'Yes.'

'Terrific.' Aleksey smiled and showed remarkable bright teeth.

'Really, I had the idea that all artists, poets, ballet dancers and actors had a tough life. It is hard to get to the top and hard to stay there.'

'I have a talent.'

'For..'

'Smoothing the path. Charm comes in useful.'

The snacks arrived and I could not help but eat most of the salmon and potato cakes as if I had fasted for a fortnight. I remembered that I had seen something about Aleksey getting an award and asked, 'What was it that you were given recently?' I omitted to tell him that I had read about this on an old copy of *Leningradskaya Pravda* whilst visiting the toilet in our block.

'I was given the award of the City's Artist this year because I have done nothing other than help portray Leningrad as full of funny characters.'

'You were quite serious in *The Flight*[32].'

---

[32] This is a 1970 Soviet historical drama film mainly based on Mikhail Bulgakov's play, The Flight. It was written and directed by Alexandr Alov and Vladimir Naumov and is the story about a group of White refuges from the Russian Civil War eking out an

'Ah, you know my work well. I do have a serious side. And what of you? What is your hidden side?'

'Oh dear, I am a simple worker. There is nothing to hide.'

'I doubt that very much and would like to find out for myself.'

'You are handsome and single; you must have a string of girlfriends.'

Aleksey took a swig of vodka and looked intently at me before saying, 'It is true, I have had a good deal of female interest and I am not proud to tell you that I have broken more than a few hearts but there comes a time in life, a time in my life at least, when I realise that I am not going to go on forever. I enjoyed my time and my loves but I don't want to get old and have only memories to keep me warm at night.' He looked at me with some intent. I was going to be flippant and say something like I imagine you say that to all the girls, but decided that he was being sincere. He then added, 'If no hidden side, what do you do?'

'I work for... no, sorry, up until today, I worked as the assistant for Professor Lebedev at the Institute of Microbiology. He decided that he could no longer employ the mother of a traitor.'

'You really have had a bad day, haven't you?' I decided that I wouldn't tell him that my father also

---

existence in Istanbul and Paris in the 1920's.

died. It might seem completely wrong that I was being light-hearted.

'Could have been worse.' I quipped. Aleksey refilled our glasses and then excused himself to use the facilities. In the short time he was away, I thought, *Today has been a bad day, that is true, but at the end I have survived and I am a changed woman. From the frightened girl who needed to be under the covers of her parents' bed to the resilient and strong woman of today. Pappa would be proud; I have sisu.*

I understood that I am also a Soviet woman, a complete Soviet product, able to cope with every condition and finding, somehow, a way of surviving. But, in being a Soviet woman, I am not without hope. Hope that tomorrow I will find something interesting in the shop, like a pineapple or banana, and hope, most of all, that I will find love.

Editor's Postscript

Hilkka died in 1999 of heart disease and we received the manuscript of her book in 2001. Although I didn't have the opportunity to talk with the author before her death, I asked Aleksey Alkohov, ahead of publication of *A Life in a Day*, for a meeting and he readily agreed. I was pleased, as I wasn't sure how much of the book to edit or whether it needed a forward or a postscript. I felt that after I had met with Aleksey it would be clearer.

Below are the notes made shortly after our meeting at his dacha.

I was warmly greeted by Aleksey on my arrival and was surprised and delighted to find that Alina, his daughter, was with him; visiting from America. I was shown to the garden and whilst waiting for Aleksey and Alina to join me I was able to take a few minutes to appreciate the delightful view.

Tolstoy would have been happy at Aleksey Alkohov's dacha. It was rustic and, in its dilapidation, utterly Russian and totally perfect. A sun-filled verandha overlooked a roughly mowed lawn that ran down to a vodka-clear stream. I admired the cascades of roses overflowing the pergolas and was tempted, but resisted the urge, to swing in a hammock that spanned two pear trees. The late August sun was strong enough for me to still need the benefit of a hat even though it filtered through leaves of the overhanging trees.

It wasn't long before Alina and Aleksey walked from the verandha, down a small flight of rocky steps, into the garden. Either side of the steps were an abundance of dahlias coming into multicoloured bloom.

Alina carried, what turned out to be, a jug of elderflower cordial, shrouded by a lace cover, and placed it on a table with chairs surrounding it under the shade of a maple tree. Aleksey brought out a platter of dried meats, bread, olives and a bottle of what he described as the wine of the gods. Under his arm he held what appeared to be a photograph album.

Although over eighty, Aleksey was upright and charming and his eyes still shone as brightly as Hilkka described in her book. Alina was tall and slender like her father but had picked up the American habit of talking too loudly. That, as far as I could make out, was her only fault. She was pretty and funny and later proved to be great hostess. When I found that she was working as a translator at Massachusetts Institute of Technology, it was obvious whom I would ask to translate *A Life in a Day*.

Aleksey asked whether I liked the garden and, when I said that I did, he explained that this had been Hilkka's passion. I remembered that she had enjoyed tending the dahlias at the Institute of Microbiology.

Conversation flowed easily. We talked of Aleksey's life in films and of the many awards he had received. I asked him, 'Of all the films that you were in, which do you think was the best?' He replied, 'I've been in many great films but the one in which I gave my best performance was definitely *No Tears for Leningrad*.' He reminded me that it had won an Academy Award for best foreign picture and he promised to show me his medal of the USSR State Prize for his role in the film when we went back into the house.

Aleksey opened the album, which he had carried into the garden and explained that this contained mostly pictured of Hilkka's family taken since 1976. In quickly flicking through the pages, I could immediately see the family features that they shared with Hilkka.

I found out that both Asta and Kristiina now lived in Helsinki and Ilona lived in Moscow with her husband who, I was informed, was known as Mr. Big in the sock world. Lotta still lived in Kanska, Siberia.

Of the four sisters, Lotta's photographs showed her to be dressed the most casually, freely even, and she often had a band of multi-coloured material platted into her hair. I wondered whether she continued her hippy lifestyle.

I am old enough to remember some of the reports of the Soviet Hippies and the System. More so now than back in the seventies, I find it odd to think that they proclaimed freedom, love and harmony at a time when most of the rest of the country dressed and thought the same. If the rest of the population expressed a view, it was satisfaction that they were part of a nation building communism and took pride in being citizens of a great power.

After we had exhausted the subject of Hilkka's sisters, we talked of Alina's life in America and about my job as Editor-in-Chief. The situation and easy conversation made for a lovely afternoon but, at the end of it, I felt nothing I'd heard needed to be added to Hilkka's book.

However, Dear Reader, I thought you might be interested in a few 'postscript' facts.

Hilkka's son, Pavel never did return to Russia and Hilkka did not see him again. He died in 1991 of AIDS. Rudolf Nureyev had not in any way been influential in Pavel's defection, but he later brought Pavel and Oleg under his wing and both starred alongside him at the London Coliseum's Nureyev Festival.

Asta had followed in her father's footsteps to become a doctor and had specialised in paediatrics. It made me wonder what professions the other sisters would have followed had the Soviets not limited their life-choices by invading Finland.

On her father's death, Hilkka had interred his ashes next to the grave of his wife in Karelia. This was with the blessing of Sonja who also asked for her ashes to be scattered on the plot at the end of her life. This was carried out as she requested and we can only assume that Pauli is now in the happy presence of his two loves.

Hilkka's ashes remain in an urn in Aleksey's apartment. She wanted to be buried with her life's love and, on his death, they will both have a memorial in the Poets, Writers and Actors graveyard in Leningrad, now renamed, St. Petersburg.

Finally, you might be interested in what became of the residence of Svetlana. The sub-division of the old apartment has gone and the whole apartment has been renovated. The entire floor is currently owned by one of the new rich. How the wheel of time slowly comes full circle!

Sergei Batalov
Editor-in-Chief
Smirnova Press

Other Relevant Publications

Article 58
By Russell John Connor

Sent from Latvia to Siberia at the age of only fifteen, this is the story of a young man's endurance, survival and love. It is set against a cruel political system that identified millions as 'enemies of the people'.

It ends on the day before Stalin's state funeral; a day which proved that from his coffin the twentieth century's most brutal dictator had not lost his capacity to deal out death at random to his subjects.

Caught in the Baltic Tide
By Russell John Connor

On the eve of the Second World War, a young Englishman suffers a serious accident in Latvia whilst working for the British electrical equipment company, Metropolitan Vickers. Unable to return home, he is witness to the unfolding war and Russian occupation. Imprisoned by the Russian State Security, he is eventually set free by his betrothed just before the arrival of the invading German army. Together, they attempt to escape the country.

Review request

Thank you for reading A Life in a Day. Please write a review to help others make a decision about choosing this book. Feedback is also very important for the author.

www.ingramcontent.com/pod-product-compliance
Lightning Source LLC
Chambersburg PA
CBHW061755020426
42331CB00006B/1487